A LOOK AT WEATHER

TORNADOES

BY KATE MIKOLEY

Gareth Stevens
PUBLISHING

CRASHCOURSE

Please visit our website, www.garethstevens.com. For a free color catalog of all our high-quality books, call toll free 1-800-542-2595 or fax 1-877-542-2596.

Cataloging-in-Publication Data

Names: Mikoley, Kate.
Title: Tornadoes / Kate Mikoley.
Description: New York : Gareth Stevens Publishing, 2024. | Series: A look at weather| Includes glossary, index, and bibliographic information
Identifiers: ISBN 9781538287408 (pbk) | ISBN 9781538287415 (library bound) | ISBN 9781538287422 (ebook)
Subjects: LCSH: Tornadoes-- Juvenile literature
Classification: LCC QC955.2 M55 2024 | DDC 551. 55/3--dc24

First Edition

Published in 2024 by
Gareth Stevens Publishing
2544 Clinton Street
Buffalo, NY 14224

Designer: Karen Quigley
Editor: Kate Mikoley

Photo credits: Cover, p. 1 solarseven/Shutterstock.com; pp. 2, 3, 31, 32 Jewelzz/Shutterstock.com; series art (warm/cold front symbols) NickJulia/Shutterstock.com; series art (cloud background) ekapol sirachainan/Shutterstock.com; series art (cartoon cloud) MimaCZ/Shutterstock.com; p. 5 AbingdonTornado/commons.wikimedia.org; p. 7 John D Sirlin/Shutterstock.com; p. 9 Eugene R Thieszen/Shutterstock.com; p. 11 Francis Lavigne-Theriault/iStockphoto.com; p. 13 mdesigner125/iStockphoto.com; p. 15 Tornado in Montana 1990 (24215082307)/commons.wikimedia.org; pp. 17, 25 clintspencer/iStockphoto.com; p. 19 File:Tornado im Bereich Henessey und Stillwater, Oklahoma, 19. Mai 2010 IX.jpg/commons.wikimedia.org; p. 19 illustration Lucky Creative/Shutterstock.com; p. 21 1925tornado-p2o-b/commons.wikimedia.org; p. 23 Trenton2011/commons.wikimedia.org; p. 27 Jeff Smith - Perspectives/Shutterstock.com; p. 29 swa182/Shutterstock.com; p. 30 Designua/Shutterstock.com.

Printed in the United States of America

CONTENTS

Words in the glossary appear in **bold** type the first time they are used in the text.

STRONG SPINNING STORMS

When a strong, spinning wind forms a cone-like shape that reaches from the clouds to the ground, you've got a tornado. These powerful storms can knock down buildings and throw cars in the air. However, most don't cause that much **damage**.

Make the Grade

Tornadoes are sometimes also called twisters.

Tornados have the strongest winds on Earth. These winds can move as fast as 300 miles (482 km) per hour. Tornadoes commonly form during **thunderstorms**. However, most thunderstorms don't result in tornadoes.

Make the Grade

Most tornadoes are over within a few minutes. However, some last for several hours.

A TWISTER FORMS

A rising movement of air is called an updraft. When winds in a thunderstorm change speed and direction, an updraft can start to rotate, or spin. The spinning updraft pulls in warm air from the thunderstorm. It gets faster, forming the tornado.

Make the Grade

When a single thunderstorm creates many tornadoes, it's called a tornado family. Many tornadoes in one area are called a tornado outbreak.

THE FUNNEL CLOUD

The cone-like shape formed by the updraft is known as a **funnel** cloud. Once the funnel cloud touches the ground, it becomes a tornado. The funnel cloud gets longer as the tornado gets stronger.

Make the Grade

After a while, the funnel cloud may appear darker. This is because the cloud has picked up dirt and **debris**.

Once a funnel cloud touches ground, it moves across land at about 30 miles (48 km) per hour. Tornadoes commonly die out when they move over colder ground. They may also die because the clouds above them have broken apart.

Make the Grade

Funnel clouds are made up of many tiny drops of water called droplets. These are what make a funnel cloud visible, or able to be seen.

WHEN AND WHERE?

Tornadoes happen all over the world. Most are reported within the United States. The Great Plains is where most U.S. tornadoes happen. This includes the Dakotas, Nebraska, and Kansas. It also includes parts of Montana, Wyoming, Colorado, Texas, Oklahoma, and New Mexico.

Make the Grade

Tornado Alley is a nickname for the part of the United States where tornadoes happen most. It covers the Great Plains plus parts of other states such as Iowa, Minnesota, and Missouri.

Tornadoes can happen at any time of the year. However, most happen during the spring or summer, when thunderstorms are most common. While they can happen at any time of day, tornadoes most commonly happen between 4 and 9 p.m.

Make the Grade

Tornadoes tend to happen later in the day because by then the sun has heated the air and ground enough to make thunderstorms form more easily.

RATING A TORNADO

Scientists use a **scale** called the **Enhanced** Fujita Scale to rate tornadoes. The scale goes from zero (EF-0) to five (EF-5). It's based on the wind speed of three-second **gusts** and damage caused by the tornado.

Make the Grade

Before 2007, the first Fujita Scale was used. A team of weather scientists reworked that scale to make the Enhanced Fujita Scale, which was put into use on February 1, 2007.

Enhanced Fujita Scale

rating	3-second gust speed
0	65-85 miles (105-137 km) per hour
1	86-110 miles (138-177 km) per hour
2	111-135 miles (178-217 km) per hour
3	136-165 miles (218-266 km) per hour
4	166-200 miles (267-322 km) per hour
5	Over 200 miles (322 km) per hour

RECORD-BREAKING TORNADOES

A 1925 tornado holds the record for farthest **distance** traveled by a single tornado. The Tri-State Tornado went through Missouri, Illinois, and Indiana. It traveled for 219 miles (352 km) and killed nearly 700 people.

Make the Grade

The Tri-State Tornado of 1925 holds the record for longest-lasting tornado too. It lasted for 3.5 hours.

The Super Outbreak of 2011 happened from April 26 to April 28. More than 300 tornadoes formed across 15 U.S. states. More than 340 people died and more were hurt. The worst of the storms' damage happened in Alabama.

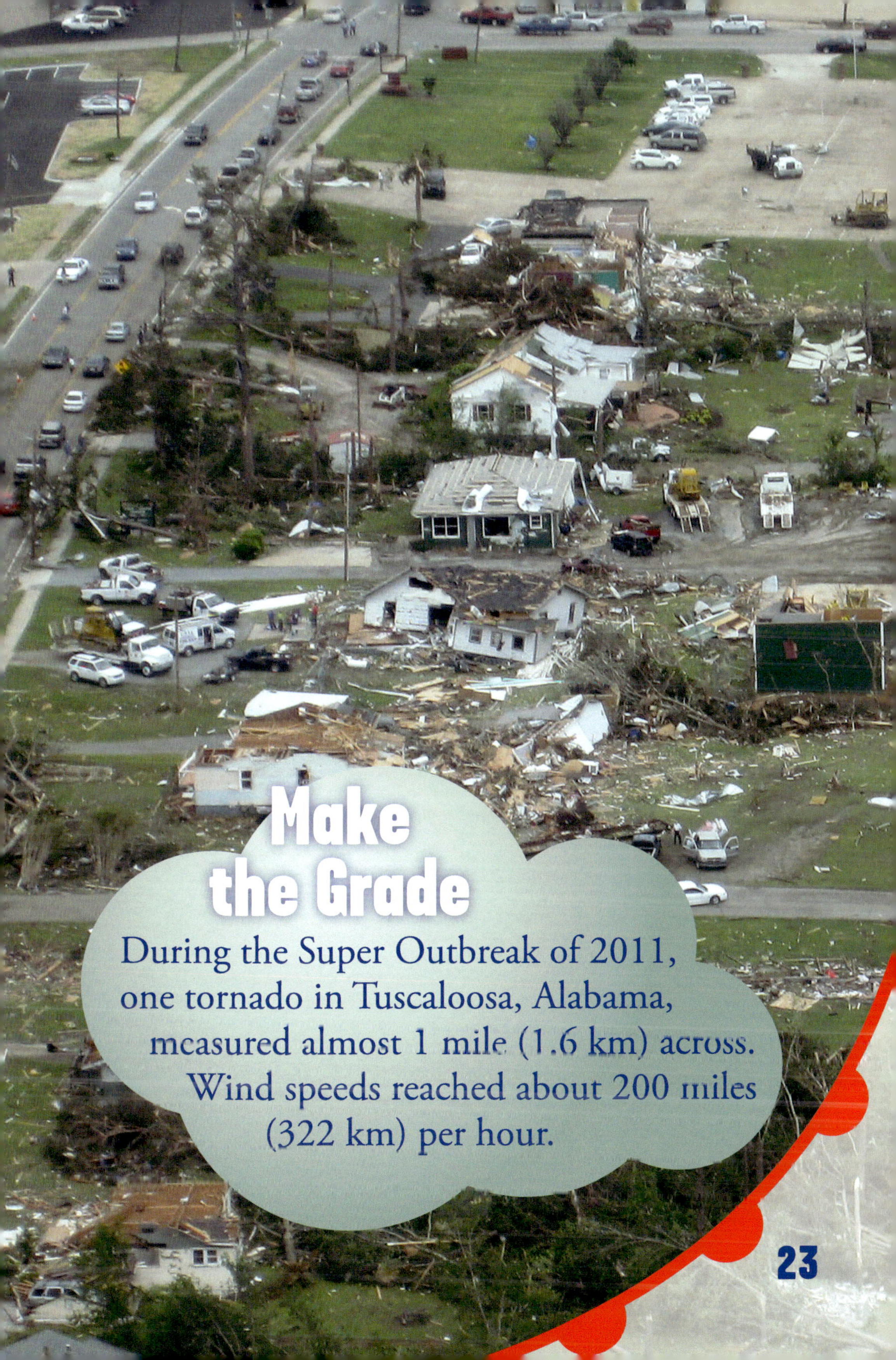

Make the Grade

During the Super Outbreak of 2011, one tornado in Tuscaloosa, Alabama, measured almost 1 mile (1.6 km) across. Wind speeds reached about 200 miles (322 km) per hour.

DANGER FROM THE STORM

Most tornadoes are over before they've traveled 6 miles (10 km). Still, they can cause lots of damage. Strong winds can destroy homes and businesses, pull trains from their tracks, and rip bark from trees.

Make the Grade

A strong enough tornado can draw up water, totally drying out a space where there once was a river.

STAYING SAFE

Scientists who study weather can often tell in advance when and where a tornado might happen. If you live in a place where a tornado might happen, it's best to have an **emergency** action plan. You can create one with your family.

Make the Grade

A tornado watch means tornadoes are possible and likely to happen in the area. A tornado warning means one has already started.

The best **shelter** for a tornado is inside a strong, **sturdy** building. A basement or room without any windows may be the safest place to be. If possible, have a kit ready with blankets, water, food, a flashlight, and a radio.

Make the Grade

If a person is caught outside in a tornado, they should stay low to the ground and lie in a ditch if possible.

FUNNEL FORMATION

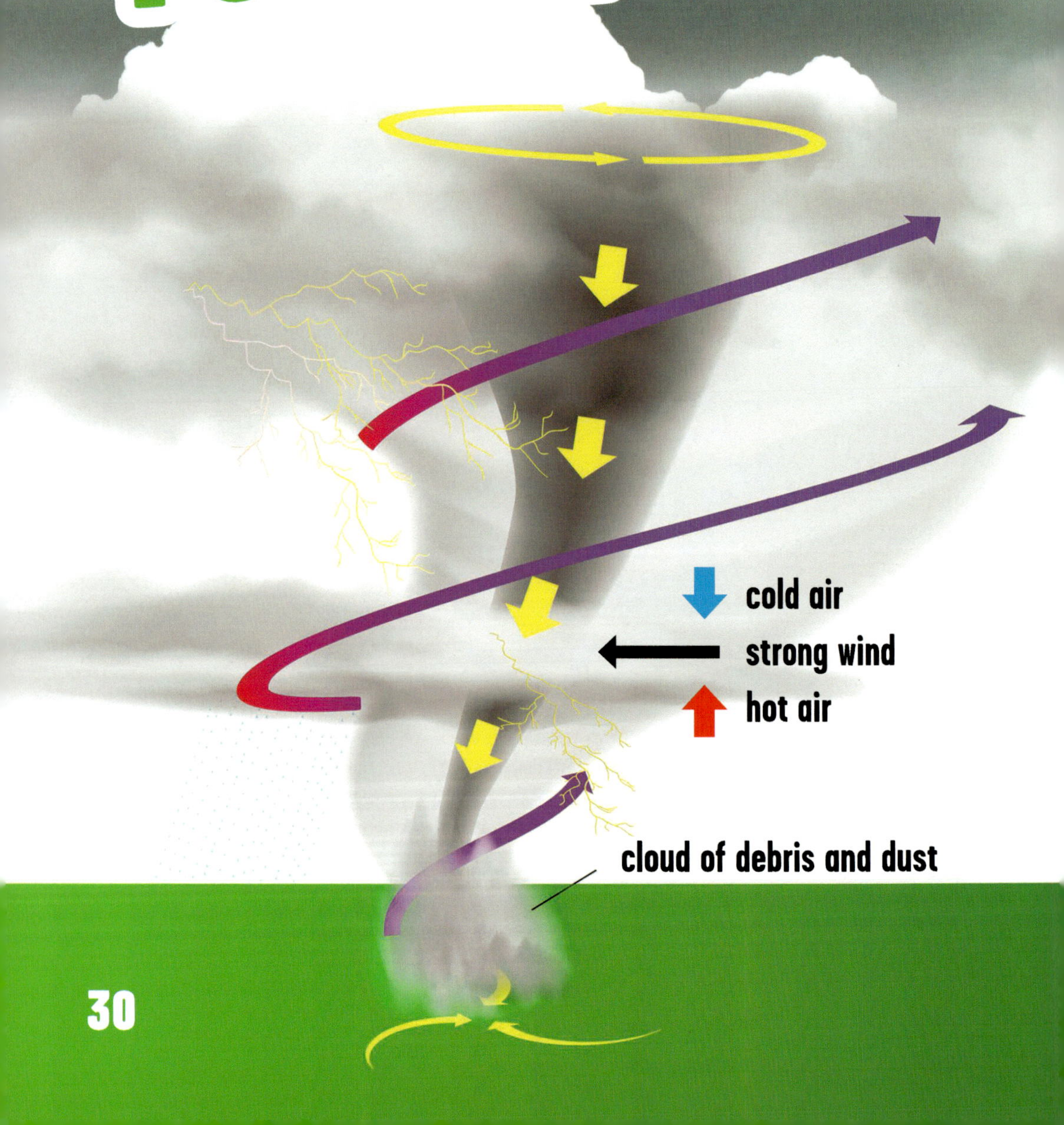

GLOSSARY

damage: Harm.

debris: Things that are lying where they fell.

distance: The space between two points.

emergency: An unexpected situation that needs quick action.

enhance: To better in value.

funnel: Something shaped like a hollow cone.

gust: A sudden, powerful rush of wind.

scale: A rating by which something can be measured.

shelter: A place where animals or people are kept safe.

sturdy: Firmly built.

thunderstorm: A storm with thunder and lightning.

FOR MORE INFORMATION

BOOKS

Farndon, John, Sean Callery, and Miranda Smith. *Weather*. New York, NY: Scholastic, 2020.

London, Martha. *Tornadoes*. Minneapolis, MN: Discover Roo, 2020.

WEBSITE

Tornadoes
kids.nationalgeographic.com/science/article/tornado
Learn more about tornadoes and see pictures of them here.

INDEX